Fallen Leaves

A Poetry Collection

Paul Budd

Speart House Publishing
Speart House
Morton Spirt
Abbots Morton
Worcestershire WR7 4LY

Copyright © Paul Budd 2018

ISBN: 978-1-911323-09-9

For Connie

who truly lights up a room

Index	Page

Index   Page

A Prayer for Mary

I see the pictures of your youth
hear your history, know the truth
how hard it was to state your case.
Love keep you safe in its embrace.

I see your children all full grown
I know your care cannot be shown
a prayer unspoken in your face.
Love keep you safe in its embrace.

Though summer fades to September
those first seasons I remember
your boundless energy and grace.
Love keep you safe in its embrace.

When you see life's mistakes repeat
as children's children find their feet
then all I wish, though commonplace.
Love keep you safe in its embrace.

If the coin of life falls heads
remember us as newly-weds
though I may leave without a trace
love keep you safe in its embrace.

Memories

I remember the beachfront at Blankenburg
reading Biggles on my first ferry trip
logs floating in the school swimming pool
diving through the bark and chippings.
I remember my first chess match.

I remember a blood red sky in February
the arboretum at Westonbirt
the grating sound of my first car when it was sold
the thirty-millimetre shell that stood on my windowsill.
I remember picking damsons.

I remember lightening over the English Channel
Dorset apple cake and mad Tom
chasing geese across a field
the first taste of a ham bap and Coca-Cola.
A dead body on the motorway.

I remember walking along to the Lighthouse
dinner at the Cottage in the Wood and climbing the Malverns
the library at Arundel Castle
watching a Spitfire swoop and soar
but most of all I remember you.

When Connie Comes to Stay

Connie comes to our house
to stay a day or two.
Nana gets things ready
and there's lots of things to do.
How will it all get done she laughs
there's so much to get through.
So all the toys together
said they'd work with Nana too.

Robin says *I'll rock a while*
with Connie on my back.
And Ellie says *I'll take her case*
and help her to unpack.
Teddington finds the Duplo box
and lays some railway track.
While Lily says *I'll slice some bread*
to make a tasty snack.

The garden and the orchard
are keen to play their part.
So they order all the bluebells
to show their purple hearts
and turn the wild orchids
into perfect works of art.
They prune and weed just everything
making all the borders smart.

Nana has a last look round
checks inside and out,
makes sure that all the snowmen
are standing straight and stout.
She thanks the toys in person
and says *there is no doubt,*
the days that Connie comes to stay
I would not do without.

A Dog's Breakfast

(with apologies to A.A.Milne)

The Greeks asked the French,
and the French asked their President
Could they have some money, they're rather in the red?
The President said, *Certainly. I'll go and ask the Eurozone.*
Now, before this hurts their cred.

The Eurozone waited
for a meeting with the Chancellor,
Could they have some money? they're running out of bread.
The Chancellor said wearily,
You'd better tell these debtors
that economists nowadays prefer austerity instead.

The Eurozone said *Fancy!*
And went to the Elysee.
Bowing to the President, reluctantly they said
Excuse us Mr President, for taking of the liberty,
but austerity's effective, if it's very thickly spread.

The President said *Oh!*
And went to see the Greeks,
as their crisis reached its head
Talking of money, many people think austerity is better.
Would you like to try some austerity instead?

The Greeks said *Bother!*
And then they said *Oh deary me!*
The Greeks sobbed *Oh deary me!*
And went back to bed.
Nobody they whimpered *could call us demanding,*
but austerity's as popular as a solid lump of lead.

The President said *There, there!*
And went to the Eurozone.
The Eurozone said *There, there!*
And went back to Germany, who said,
There, there! We didn't really mean it.
Here's money for the Greeks; to the Eurozone we're wed.

The Greeks took the money and brought it to their parliament.
The Greeks said *Money eh?* and bounced out of bed.
Nobody they said, as they counted very carefully,
Nobody they said, as they checked with solicitors,
Nobody, dear Europe, would call us demanding,
BUT we do have a credit rating that's now double zed.

What the Telecoms Website Told Me

That:

I can't telephone them to complain
enquiries through the website will be dealt with in three days,
my complaint needs to fall into one of five headings
that if I choose the wrong heading I will need to start again.

That:

my complaint doesn't fall into any of their categories,
customer service is important to them
they will not tolerate inappropriate language.
That while I'm waiting for a reply I might like to consider their
new broadband options.

That:

I don't live in an area where broadband speed supports those
options,
their website will be closing in five minutes for essential
maintenance,
they apologise for the interruption in service and will I resubmit
my complaint.
That more people than ever are choosing Telecoms as their
service provider.

That they are sorry to lose my business but look forward to
welcoming me back at any time.

City Life

How to describe my pinstriped working day?
The barren desk the barb of office spite.
Saharan days pursuing Mammon's pay
wire-locked time before the freeing night.

Sometimes, by chance, I glimpse hope's golden ray,
cloudless sunlit sky sheds a clearer light
a beacon flashing out a better way
a siren call to cease the daily fight.

And then I know that magic time will come
when you and I my love are truly free.
Rose-scented garden time denied to some
those stone-crushed lives lost earning Charon's fee.

As long as we're together, you and I,
our hopes, our dreams, our love, will never die.

A Hundred Years

How does it feel to live a hundred years?
To be born when the world was waging war
sharing life's fleeting joys and blinding tears.

Your seasons turn but a steady line steers
a course through the days and months: nature's law.
How does it feel to live a hundred years?

Time stretched beyond that dwindling band of peers
the ceaseless cull of those that you adore
sharing life's fleeting joys and blinding tears.

Did you watch your children grow see their fears,
ease their woes, teach them how to keep the score?
How does it feel to live a hundred years?

Does God watch over you, patient as he hears
your prayers? Did you learn what time was for?
Sharing life's fleeting joys and blinding tears?

I want to know, as the fog of life clears,
while you stand close on death's iron shore.
How does it feel to live a hundred years
sharing life's fleeting joys and blinding tears?

A Tailored Jacket

I'm sure it was there this morning.
I put it down beside the bed.
But I have this thought that's dawning
going round and round my aged head.

It's not the first time it's been lost
it took an age to find before
I'm not worried about the cost
but how it stuck beneath the door.

An hour working out how to free it.
Jammed hard between the door and floor,
I wasn't sure I could save it:
spine broke, its condition poor.

I considered ironing the pages
weighting it down with other books.
But decided that would take ages
and why judge a book by its looks?

A Plague on Beanstalks

Not easy being twelve feet tall:
you hit your head on every door.
For us it's twice as far to fall
upon an unforgiving floor.

So the wife and I found a place
away from all the stress and strife.
Protected by a sheer cliff face
we built a simple, peaceful, life.

One day this pesky midget came
clambering up a giant stalk.
Taking pity on him all the same
my wife and he began to talk.

This worm wheedled and cajoled,
spoke long about: his widowed mum,
her poverty, the cow he'd sold,
but then he heard my fee fo fum.

Full tilt I chased him from the house.
Outside, he darted for the edge.
I really thought I'd caught the louse
as he paused upon a ledge.

I grabbed my ladder, once so trusty,
now to my complete despair
I found its rungs were rusty.
Who said life is just or fair?

I tested out the vegetation
to see if it would hold my weight,
then climbed down in agitation
to seal the little blighter's fate.

But halfway down I heard a rip
the beanstalk started to give way.
The angle steep, I lost my grip
and plunged down into the bay.

Of the worm's fate I cannot tell
he'd fled, ending our short thriller
but my reputation grew as well
they call me *the beanstalk killer*.

Basil Thompson

The day 'T' for Tommy took to the sky
cameras instead of bombs plotting its course,
heading eastwards, rain drumming on glass,
was that when strange voices began to call?
Hamburg voices? Bombed, burnt and broken souls
splintering like shrapnel into the night.

Evil, red, hungry flames burning all night
three thousand feet of scorching, warping sky
monument to those fifteen thousand souls.
Essential to the war effort of course
a sharp, vital, bloody clarion call.
As you flew by the nation raised a glass.

What pierced you through the camera's cold glass?
Lingering visions of that killing night?
frame after frame to prove that death may call
killing children out of a jet-black sky?
They were collateral damage of course
deaths we purchased at the cost of your souls.

You were cursed with one of those gentle souls,
a caring, beating heart, not made of glass.
Nothing the airforce could have known of course.
A simple mission, just another night
flying out to a hostile German sky
to satisfy a war-torn nation's call.

Was success' measure far too close to call?
Scales unbalanced by all those tormented souls?
When you were back above a British sky
your reflection caught in unforgiving glass
dead eyes revealing the abyss of night
did you sense your troubled mind changing course?

Or was there then a bitter second course
when you answered Britain's bleak mission call
and flew once more into a burning night?
A firestorm of one hundred thousand souls
proud Dresden captured through your camera glass.
A city turned to ashes in the sky.

Thrown off course you heard through that burning sky
madness call as loud as shattering glass
join me this night and silence those troubled souls.

Catching a Train

I just need to get on a train
I'll disappear to the west coast of Scotland
for a few days, perhaps a week.
Get away from it all, regroup.

I'll disappear to the west coast of Scotland
watch those sunsets across to Skye.
Get away from it all, regroup,
breathe the fresh air leave the stale behind.

Watch those sunsets across to Skye
a change from the City smoke
breathe the fresh air leave the stale behind.
Maybe walk along the beach.

A change from the City smoke
for a few days, perhaps a week,
maybe walk along the beach.
I just need to get on a train.

Tribute to Henry V on the 600th Anniversary of Agincourt

Hear me,
all those that doubt.
Don't fear the coming day,
or dread the name of Agincourt.
Stand firm.
Six hundred years from now they'll talk
about St. Crispin's Day,
and acclaim your
Victory!

City Smoke

I stand before your picture on the wall
an office setting somewhere in the smoke
a pinstripe broker standing proud and tall.

We seldom met alone and scarcely spoke
kept our distance - divisions too great
to be bridged, not until your second stroke.

I knew by then, of course, it was too late.
That was the darkened evening of your time
sand-built foundations swept away by fate.

Strange then to watch you end your social climb
all that striving, grabbing, grinding. Time shed
playing out your city pantomime.

Had we spoken then what would I have said?
For as I see you there in black and white,
buried now, it was then that you were dead.

This Summer

Scenting heavy perfumed pine this summer
grapes taken straight from vine this summer.

Walking ancient hedge-bound rights of way
guided by the acorn sign this summer.

Chasing butterflies, champagne flutes in hand
drinking ice cool vintage wine this summer.

Hanging baskets draped on white brick walls,
sweet peas growing in a line this summer.

Glimpsing cloud-cradled moon and evening stars
sensing heavenly design this summer.

Touching sun warmed stones and gentle grass
holding hands and feeling fine this summer.

The greater gift for Paul than all of these,
knowing, Mary, you are mine this summer.

'This Summer' first published in Tarriance
by Stratford Scribes, July 2017

Creative Selling

Concise Oxford Dictionary,
reasonably good condition.
English, standard stationery,
approved for all tuition.
Treasure for a visionary,
ideal for word technician.
Vital crossword accessory.
Essential first edition.

Escape

Across the Aegean Sea
a million souls will cross.
From oppression they flee
across the Aegean Sea
to a land they know is free.
Despite the countless loss,
across the Aegean Sea
a million souls will cross.

Crimea

I read about the light brigade
their lives, their deaths, their cavalcade.
Saw pictures of a bygone age
but never thought at any stage
that modern Russia would invade.

Journalists found it hard to gauge
the passion or the Russian's rage
or even where to find Crimea
Sevastopol or somewhere near
where they could write that telling page.

Politicians were quite unclear
should Ukraine, or the West, now fear
the coming of another war?
For what else might be held in store
with Russian troops at their frontier?

They thought best to forget, ignore
Ukraine had surely known the score
Europe's interest lay elsewhere
and no one in the West would dare
to fight a deadly Russian war.

So those in Independence Square
who fought for all that's just and fair
left families, homes, or even paid
in blood or life will be betrayed
when we forget the whole affair.

Customer Service

You posted our cheque books to an address that wasn't there
played us endless jingles that said you really care
sent out forms to fill a hundred pages long
said they were the right ones. You were completely wrong.
You lent out our money as freely as the air
charged us massive fees that no one thought were fair.
Your lending was reckless it almost brought us down,
and made of syndication a dreadful complex noun.
Scottish independence would have brought your problems South.
We hear all that you're saying but trust nothing from your mouth.
Through all the years of pain the strife that you have caused
your stream of massive bonuses has never even paused.
We had to underwrite for you a hundred billion pounds
in return our animosity knows no real bounds.

First Born

I come from a family in sorrow
a home overwhelmed by loss
a mantelpiece full of condolence cards,
children's clothes marked 'for charity.'

I come from a family that didn't understand
the death of a child or how to grieve.
Of relatives unable to reach and support
young parents closed off from the world.

I come from a family that moved home
to escape from it all
who began with a fresh start, again and again,
amongst strangers; strange houses, strange towns.

I come from a family in crisis
where I believed I was the firstborn.

New Foundations

I am from a land of new estates
chip sharp rockeries and broken wheelbarrows
bagged peat, rotted manure and roses.

I am from a land of cool cement
smelling of paint, drying plaster,
fresh sawn timber, new laid bricks.

I am from a land of new neighbours
new friends, new bicycles, new games,
carpets not to be played on
polished parquet to slide on.

I am from a land of designated days
fishmonger Wednesday, grocer Saturday,
butcher's boy Monday, Lyons' cakes Friday.

I am from a land of numbers
Halliwell's at number ten,
Millington's at number three,
us at number fourteen.

I am from a land of ratepayers
Rotarians, Women's Institute,
Church and roast on Sundays.

I am from a land where every day is new
and the past is elsewhere.

Real News

I believe that politicians start out with good intentions
that once upon a time we had an advanced democracy
that the Higgs Boson really does exist
that there probably was life on Mars
that Apollo 11 really did land on the moon
that Elvis Presley is dead
that Lee Harvey Oswald killed JFK
that Shakespeare wrote his own plays
that Adolf Hitler died in 1945
that Syria uses chemical weapons
that Donald Trump was elected President
that Brexit is a mess
I believe that good is stronger than evil.

The Heart of Poets

In the beginning of the earth
until the very edge of time
absent from man's dominion
but present in his rhyme
I am always to be found
in the struggling poet's heart
but never to be seen
as the essence of his art.

I Saw

I saw
I saw
I saw
I saw
I saw
I saw
kindling

A Tick Box World

Tick a box. Tick male. Tick white. Tick English. Tick weight at
birth and school of choice. Tick qualifications. Tick married. Tick
children. Tick employed. Tick homeowner. Tick car. Tick benefits.
Tick insurance. Tick non-smoker, drinker, debts, mobile, e-mail.
Tick pension. Tick over eighty. Tick political donation. Tick made
a gift in the last seven years. Tick flowers or charity. Tick
executor. Tick coffin. Tick oak or pine. Tick burial. Tick if you
don't want e-marketing. Tick Mastercard or Visa.

In Praise of the Plays of William Shakespeare

Soft, what words of magic these,
that do trip so light and gentle
from a mortal's pen?

Verily is the writer's winter
made glorious spring by this
bard of Stratford.
His writing be the solace of kings,
read on, give me chapter after chapter.

For it is nobler to suffer
the seating at the Swan
than suffer outrageous talent shows,
or sit once more before the
television to watch Friends,
or listen close to the English news.

For in the evening nothing so
becomes a man as a stirring play
stiffening the sinews against hard upholstery,
and paying for the tickets an earthly fortune.

Keeping in Touch

I don't know if he wants to talk to me
we parted on something of a sour note.
I'm in a much better place now
I'm having counselling for the drugs and the booze.

We parted on something of a sour note
he should know I'm in a new relationship.
I'm having counselling for the drugs and booze
and the baby's due around late June.

He should know I'm in a new relationship
I've got a house with Carly
and the baby's due around late June.
I've sold the mobile home and left the past behind.

I've got a house with Carly.
I'm in a much better place now
I've sold the mobile home and left the past behind.
I don't know if he wants to talk to me.

Commuting

Iron, metal, plastic, spring,
balanced on a dancing string.
Feet, clay-bound, rooted
body still, dark blue suited
Streaming doors, stilted voice
Mind the gap! there is no choice.
Twisted left, flung far right.
Stolen platforms lost from sight.
Garlic breath, worried faces.
Briefcase perched in empty spaces.
Oyster cards, lobster trains
sallow flesh and sombre strains.
Nine to five, clock in sight.
Peacock blue of City night.
Electric hiss, frenzied, rushed,
city life, draining, crushed.

Loss

He died at nineteen
a motorbike accident
just one of those things
a wet road, a tricky bend
a little too fast.
Hit an oncoming lorry.

He had a helmet
wore leathers, the bike was new
bought for his birthday.
Was it only twelve months ago?

He was at Uni
not Oxbridge as they had hoped
but solid redbrick.
They thought he had a girlfriend
but don't have her name.
He didn't talk about her
just said she was nice.

They would like to get in touch
but do not know how
and there is not that much time
the funeral's next week.
They decided no flowers

no summer for their winter.

Margaret Jane

Twenty hidden years, *twenty* hidden years
a different time, a different place.
Amber trapped in black and white
she stares at me this unknown face.

A stranger in my mother's arms
no pencilled name no telling date,
a pumpkin face with snowman's eyes.
Who is she? asks my sister Kate.

We find them in the living room,
the photo in my outstretched palm.
Dull curtains drawn, cold silence falls.
I break the years of settled calm.

My father lifts tobacco eyes
my mother kneels granite-still.
The gas fire hisses, sighs and spits,
but can't dispel the growing chill.

You had a sister, Margaret Jane.
She died when you were four months' old.
We never overcame the loss.
That's why you've never been told.

How? Why? Unbidden questions flood.
The gas fire growls its urgent light.
My father turns toward his wife,
a waxen image locked in fright.

Too soon, too much, no more, enough!
Guilt floods in toxic acid streams
corroding any chance of truth.
Margaret Jane will haunt my dreams.

The Campaign

Campaigners sweep down like hawks on their prey,
carrying their banners *Vote to Leave Vote to Stay*.
The shine in their eyes is like sparks from a blaze
that burns in their hearts like a fevered malaise.

Like a swarm from the hive when the summer is high
descending en masse to wherever they spy
a voter out shopping, or a chance to impress
with a soundbite on Facebook or soapbox address.

For the voice of the people demands to be heard.
From those clever and knowing to the downright absurd,
a democracy stands by majority's will.
To harvest their votes requires cunning and skill.

For those wanting to leave there's no fear of decline
controlling our borders and holding the line,
reducing our numbers, protecting our race,
is noble and decent and not a disgrace.

Those wanting to stay talk of jobs and careers.
They have no interest in immigrant fears.
In relation to Brussels they have no concern
it's simply a question of waiting your turn.

But the widow of truth is down on her knees
feeling around her the lies on the breeze,
an absence of facts and a rising despair
for staying or leaving she no longer cares.

Safe in England I sit

I watch the election   in the United States
Donald Trump, Republican   Hillary Clinton, Democrat
seeking to build walls,   in a divided America,
appealing to the disaffected   seeking to hide a past
haters of the establishment   in Washington's ivory towers,
often misquoted,   or merely misunderstood
hard to imagine such   an uninspiring choice

as President of the United States

On the Slate

Safe in your Welsh mountain home
it took an explosion to prise you loose
a cold chisel to break you apart
a diamond saw to cut you down to size

You were annoyed
grey and cold
wanting to wipe things clean
saying we should chalk it up to experience

It was then you hit the roof
a first night on the tiles
with four thousand eight hundred friends
nails holding you east and west

When they loosened their grip
you started the long slide.
No one could stop your fall
before you ended broken in the gutter.

Sleeping on the Roadside

Sleeping on the roadside
she turned a head or two
blonde hair in my headlights
moist with morning dew

She spoke about her husband
a man of fifty-two.
She fired up a Gauloise
then asked me what to do.

Through pouting, moistened lips
of cherry ripened hue
she mouthed those fatal words,
I need a man like you.

As she spoke of freedom
her eyes turned icy blue.
And when she said she loved me
I hoped that it was true.

Nathan's a wealthy man
but he and I are through.
I deserve a better life.
My future is with you.

He is pure scum, a louse
a man of violence too.
I'm his only legal heir
I'll share his wealth with you.

I left her by the roadside
and wondered what to do.
I should have called the police
and told them all I knew.

But the fire of my passion
I couldn't now subdue.
Nor could I live without her,
I'd see the whole thing through.

I bought myself a gun
six rounds of ammo too.
I sat outside their house,
then shot the bastard through.

But when I went to find her
at our normal rendezvous
she was nowhere to be seen
and she'd told the boys in blue.

I fired my last four shots
then took a hit or two.
Now that I've been wasted
she'll set her sights on you.

Suis je Charlie?

To draw to show us all that's vain
to write but never fear disdain
to speak when others have no voice
to prize above their lives this choice.
Ils sont Charlie.

To publish the satanic verses
disregard religious curses
promote the dream of black with white
to win the vote or stop the fight.
Ils sont Charlie.

To refuse to see the world unfed
to treat the sick, to tend the dead
to risk disease they know can slay
a hundred people every day.
Ils sont Charlie.

But I, who sit here at my desk
watching slaughter, grim, grotesque,
am never put to such a test,
just live a life that's free and blessed.
Suis je Charlie?

Mud

Christmas
in the trenches
no turkey and wine, just
bully beef, McConnachie stew
and mud.

Germans
singing carols
sharing schnapps and bratwurst.
Christmas trees along the trenches
and mud.

Cold nights
supply parcels
letters from a sweetheart
but not like Christmases at home.
Just mud.

The End of the Holiday

Gazing up in dark night to silvered moon
I leave the shrimp nets where we played.
Our holidays will finish all too soon
no more time for buckets, sand or spade.
We spent happy days in chasing tiger
flew to the planets in my magic chair
climbed trees, forded streams, scaled the Eiger,
fought mighty wars with courage, skill and flair.
Now the moon sinks as gently as my heart
its beauty light and hope now lost to cloud.
Tomorrow the new school term will start
my carefree childhood trapped within its shroud.
But in my youthful way I will ever find
imaginary friends to free my mind.

The Street Piano

I hear a soft piano strain,
see a bloody pavement stain,
watch the pianist sob and cry
as armed troops mass beside the Seine
a reply to terror's reign.
I hear the muted question: why
is this world no longer sane?
answers that are sought in vain.
Why did all those people die?

Tears in the Desert

In their allotted time together magic
sparked radiant fire as bright as diamonds
across dunes made green by forgotten tears
lighting up the once lonely desert
with the power of love that used to shine
before their spell flickered, died, and was lost.

Beams that led the way have now been lost.
Yesterday she bathed in lamplit magic
as love's rose-glazed lantern yearned to shine
alchemy that turned coal into diamonds.
Now there is no wand to light the desert
or wizard's laughter to chase away the tears.

She pulls the duvet close dries martyred tears
tells herself she's young that all is not lost.
There are oases in barren desert
places she can work her kind of magic.
She sleeps at last to dream of diamonds,
Camelot princes, crystal shoes that shine.

Her pillow warms to apple-crisp sun shine.
She traces patterns made by inkblot tears,
pale dropped shadows of ice flat diamonds,
obituaries of dreams that were lost
in the night, and remembers the magic
recaptured from the bleakness of desert.

Rising from the bed she leaves the desert
behind and hoping her spirit will shine
showers waterfall tresses with magic,
stares at the steam veiled mirror. No more tears
can she find there for the love she has lost.
Flinted eyes flash brighter than diamonds.

Today is the day she will find diamonds
in every stone-dry corner of desert
no lasting regrets for what has been lost.
For today is a new day that will shine
like white silver banishing sorrowful tears.
Hers is a world of wonder and magic.

Now star-flecked magic flashes like diamonds
chasing away the tear shadowed desert
making her shine and forget what's been lost.

The Ballad of Martin Bell

This tale I'll tell of Martin Bell
a tragic life it's true.
His ending seemed unjust as well
to everyone who knew.

When he was four his father died
he overdosed on gin.
The parish chest would not provide
as funds were very thin.

To school he went fuelled on gruel,
dressed in charity wear.
He felt uncool, the boys were cruel.
He often knew despair.

As Martin grew he seldom knew
the finer things in life.
Money due meant fancies few,
no chance to take a wife.

At forty-five his mother died
her life of strife was done.
Bereft of hope poor Martin cried.
He went to buy a gun.

He sat on Beacon hill all night
his mother's shade close by.
She would have said *it's time to fight
you cannot let things lie.*

Back home he found the bailiff's man,
the landlord's rent was due.
He spied the gun in Martin's hand
and said *We'll sell that too.*

He took the gun from Martin's palm,
as he did it fired.
Although he hadn't meant him harm
the bailiff's man expired.

Poor Martin's fate was in the hands
of twelve good men and true.
Four hundred packed the courtroom stands
they filled the hallways too.

The jury heard the bailiff's wife
they saw her one young son.
She called on them for Martin's life,
they saw the fateful gun.

The judge was bored and past his prime
his voice was clipped and dry.
This was an evil, heinous crime.
I sentence you to die.

They hanged him from the gallows tree
an end to Martin's woes.
The hangman came to take his fee
and left him to the crows.

They say the bailiff's ghost is seen
declaiming Martin's fate.
This wasn't how it should have been,
but now it is too late!

The Canvasser

May I ask how you're planning to vote?
The election is soon, as you probably know
we want to ensure that we strike the right note.

We're ahead in the polls already, you'll note,
but canvassing shows it's too early to crow.
May I ask how you're planning to vote?

It's often been said that we're all in one boat
it's important, you know, to go with the flow.
We want to ensure that we strike the right note.

Our cause is one we are keen to promote
support for our side is beginning to grow.
May I ask how you're planning to vote?

The prospect of losing is really remote
but we can't be complacent you see. So
we want to ensure that we strike the right note.

The line about Hitler was just a misquote
our opponents have stooped incredibly low.
May I ask how you're planning to vote?
We want to ensure that we strike the right note.

The First World War

The First World War in black and white
a million men now lost from sight.
Marked on every village green
monuments to what might have been
were they not called upon to fight

The First World War.

A generation shining bright
symbolic of their nation's might.
Poised to vent all Europe's spleen
they could not know that it would mean
a tinder spark that would ignite

The First World War.

The mindless horror stays despite
endless wars, our financial plight,
our arguments that flow unseen
making fools of us who haven't seen
that none of it was ever quite:

The First World War

The Mountain

It was his own special space
up there in the mountain
under a sky too bright to be blue.
He found that it helped make things clear
helped his thoughts dance like a river
clearing away any deepening clouds.

It was too easy to allow the clouds
to colour his life invade his space
as each day he commuted, crossing the river
to join battle with the paperwork mountain
that seemed both impossible to clear
and determined to turn him blue.

The secret was not to be blue
to banish any hint of clouds
to keep his thoughts upbeat and clear
keep negativity from invading his space
however high the mountain
or however deep the river.

The thread that ran through his life like a river
its water sparkling and blue
fresh sprung from high on the mountain
way up as high as the clouds
where the Earth meets with space
and everything is crystal clear.

No easy task that was clear
his life more stagnant pool than running river,
impossible to find the space
and time to avoid the inner blue
or the horizon's heavy clouds
that obscured the safety of his mountain.

But each weekend he made for the mountain
climbed the high path when it was clear
kept a wary eye out for clouds,
forded the stream, more waterfall than river,
to altitudes of unfamiliar blue
to perch upon his special space.

From the mountain he watched his life's river
running clear, sometimes grey, sometimes blue,
flowing beneath the clouds and into space.

The Wine Cellar

In her youth she tasted Matteus Rosé.
At university it was vin de table,
at home it was a nouveau Beaujolais
then she discovered Haut Medoc.

The difference of a classic red
came as quite a shock,
after wines of mediocrity
she sampled Merlot, Gamay and Hock.

By her mid-twenties
she had moved from red to white
preferring over Chardonnay
Sauvignon Blanc's specific bite.

But now she's in her thirties
and money is quite tight
she goes for super savers
even though the quality is…

        not quite what it might have been.

The Lutine Bell

Sound the Lutine Bell
another ship is lost
beneath the ocean swell.
Sound the Lutine Bell
strike its dark metallic shell
and count the human cost.
Sound the Lutine Bell
another ship is lost.

The Writer

There was a young writer from Crieff
who used to write by the sheaf
she ran out of ink
and started to think
that perhaps it was quite a relief.

Yeoman at the Tower

This autumn they've been ignoring us
watching instead the poppies float
and spread across the emerald moat,
silent crowds, no noise or fuss.
A tribute to those who died for us.
I fought for country and for Queen
served my time and earnt my place
amongst the scarlet gartered race
that guard the jewels, the green,
and this, the finest sight I've ever seen.

Water

I watch her boat tilt and sink
she's only six and I'm in charge.
I gauge the intervening rocks
With tide high current running hard.

She's only six and I'm in charge
we should have known the boat's unsafe
with tide high current running hard.
She should have worn a rubber ring.

We should have known the boat's unsafe
the water's pouring in.
She should have worn a rubber ring.
I cling frozen to the harbour wall.

The water's pouring in.
I gauge the intervening rocks.
I cling frozen to the harbour wall.
I watch her boat tilt and sink.

Home Abandoned

These are all the things that surrounded you:
old-fashioned flock wallpaper, peeling, grey,
thin blue silk curtains cutting out the view
always drawn against the intruding day.

There was a time when all these things were new.
Even the Dresden clock on its metal tray
would once have had a hand or two
marking life not measuring its decay.

There are the leather slippers worn to fit
those feet for all those painful years alone,
set close to the log fire you never lit
beneath the China lamp that seldom shone.

Standing here despite the clues on view
I cannot tell when life abandoned you.

When Connie Went to Warwick Castle

It was the most beautiful day
when Nana asked *what shall we do?*
Perhaps we'll go to the castle
it's too far to go to the zoo.

They set off to Warwick by car
Connie safely strapped in her seat
sitting up close by the window
kicking Nana's chair with her feet.

They parked the car by the entrance
and took an umbrella just in case.
Nana paid for their tickets
a broadening smile on her face.

The gate was an ominous turnstile
quite as high was Connie was tall.
She slid through a gap to the side
then waited for Nana and Paul

The guide said *Knights all wore metal.*
They must have been terribly sore
bristling full of old weapons
with armour from ceiling to floor.

Relieved to be outside once more
away from the castle so dark
Nana made first for the river
then Connie caught sight of the park.

Hiding behind trees and bushes
Connie tried hard not to speak.
As she later explained to Nana
she's expert in both hide and seek.

When Connie had found everybody
they headed along to the lake.
Peacocks were fanning their feathers
they gave them a really good shake.

Connie ran round in a circle
as three ducks came up with a quack.
She chased them down through the gardens
and followed them all the way back

They stopped a while by the castle
where a crowd was standing quite still,
then gasped as Rosie the condor
swooped down from the top of the hill.

It was time to take a refreshment
so they raced to get to the shop
where Connie bought an ice lolly,
so much nicer than cola or pop.

Connie spoke to her Nana,
as her batteries started to slow
you need to plug in my charger
I can show you where it must go

She pointed out a small socket
that was buried deep in her hair.
A big surprise to her Nana
who hadn't known it was there.

So Nana plugged in the charger
urging the current to flow.
It took no more than three minutes
before Connie started to glow.

Connie came round with a flourish
telling her Nana it meant
that now her battery levels
were reaching thirty percent.

Nana will always remember
taking Connie out, so to speak.
A wonderful time at the Castle
and learning to play hide and seek.

Wheels

His first is Japanese.

A four by four that was once his mother's.
He trades it in. *Wheels* he says.
I need decent wheels.

The second is an indeterminate saloon.
Red. Fast. Short lived.
It stays on the drive, unclean,
rusting, missing vital parts.

An accumulation of points,
a summons, a ban.
A peaceful twelve months.

The third is something sensible
a small car with different coloured panels.
One wheel is smaller than the others.
Unlike the car, his money has been waxed.

The fourth is bought with his grandmother's money.
Grey, turbocharged. He thinks it is the
nicest car he's ever had.
The ban comes quicker. Lasts longer.

Abandoned cars litter his drive
decent wheels are hard to find he says.

Why Can't I Remember?

I can see the questions in their faces
it puzzles them as it puzzles me
why can't I remember names and places?

Who are these women who tie my laces
and ask me if I'm ready for some tea?
I can see the questions in their faces.

They've packed some bags or are they cases?
What's her name is going to come with me.
Why can't I remember names and places?

They all want to take their last embraces
they say that I'll be fine but can't agree.
I can see the questions in their faces.

The car doors shut, the engine races
and I wonder where I've left my key?
Why can't I remember names and places?

They say it's lovely here no airs or graces.
I don't know where I am. I'm all at sea.
I can see the questions in their faces.
Why can't I remember names and places?

Winter

I love the snow to fall in winter
to hear its icy call in winter.

Watching cotton-heavy crystal flakes
floating then drift and squall in winter.

Staring out at white hypnotic skies
holding all of us in thrall in winter.

Touching freezing ice-locked windows
wrapped up and feeling small in winter.

Fires of cracking logs and red-hot coals
indulging in a settee sprawl in winter.

Hearing choirs, singing Christmas carols,
eating from the chestnut stall in winter.

For Paul the joyous task of cutting
holly to deck the hall in winter.

www.ingramcontent.com/pod-product-compliance
Lightning Source LLC
Chambersburg PA
CBHW071851020426
42331CB00007B/1962